Mummies

Aaron Frisch

CREATIVE EDUCATION

Published by Creative Education
P.O. Box 227, Mankato, Minnesota 56002
Creative Education is an imprint of
The Creative Company
www.thecreativecompany.us

Design and production by
Christine Vanderbeek
Art direction by **Rita Marshall**
Printed in the United States of America

Photographs by Alamy (AF Archive,
Moviestore Collection Ltd, Photos 12),
Fotosearch, Getty Images (Comstock
Images, Kenneth Garrett, Purestock,
Universal Pictures/Archive Photos),
iStockphoto (Jean Assell), Shutterstock
(Goran Bogicevic, Andrew Buckin,
Rachelle Burnside, Mikhail, Dudarev
Mikhail), Veer (James Griehaber,
Richard Kegler)

**Library of Congress
Cataloging-in-Publication Data**
Frisch, Aaron.
Mummies / Aaron Frisch.
p. cm. —— (That's spooky!)
Includes bibliographical references
and index.
Summary: A basic but fun exploration of
mummies—preserved corpses that may
be revived—including how they come to
exist, their weaknesses, and memorable
examples from pop culture.
ISBN 978-1-60818-247-3
1. Mummies—Juvenile literature. I. Title.

GN293.F75 2013
393'.3—dc23   2011051179

First edition
9 8 7 6 5 4 3 2 1

CONTENTS

IMAGINE ...

You are in a museum late at night. You hear a heavy stone moving. Then you hear a moaning sound. Suddenly, you see a body wrapped in **BANDAGES** reaching out for you!

IT'S A MUMMY!

WHAT IS A MUMMY?

A mummy is a dead body that is **PRESERVED**. Mummies may be thousands of years old. Many mummies are from a country called Egypt. A mummy becomes spooky when it gets up and walks around!

Many mummies were carefully wrapped in cloth

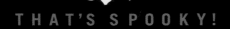

BECOMING A MUMMY

Mummies are usually buried in **TOMBS**.
Later, they might be put in a museum.
A **CURSE** can make a mummy wake up.
Taking something that belongs to a
mummy can make it mad, too.

Some mummy tombs are inside huge pyramids

8

MUMMY BEHAVIOR

Mummies chase people who steal from them. They might try to hurt people who bother their tomb. Sometimes a curse makes a mummy chase people for hardly any reason at all!

You do not want to have a mummy mad at you

A Mummy's Powers

Mummies are hard to stop. You can't kill them, because they are already dead! Mummies never get tired. And they always seem to know where to find people.

Mummies can be very strong for being old and dead

A MUMMY'S WEAKNESSES

Mummies are slow. They have stiff legs and arms. The best way to stop a mummy is to find a way to break the curse or to give the mummy back its stuff. Then the mummy will lie down again!

Bandages and old age make mummies move slowly

FAMOUS MUMMIES

Two movies called *The Mummy* are about a mummy named Imhotep. One movie is black-and-white, and one is in color. Imhotep starts to walk when a man finds his tomb and reads a **SPELL**.

The Mummy came out in 1932 and again in 1999

People like to learn about real-life mummies, too. King Tut was a king in Egypt. He died more than 3,000 years ago and was made into a mummy. King Tut has a famous gold mask that is in a museum.

Some rich Egyptian kings were buried in fancy masks

WRAP YOURSELF UP

Mummies cannot really walk around. They come to life only in spooky stories. But you can be your own mummy. Wrap yourself up in white bandages or tissues and hold your arms out straight. Then moan like you are super old!

A quick wrap can instantly make a mummy of you

moaning mouth

really old body

loose bandages

stiff arms

THAT'S SPOOKY!

LEARN TO SPOT A MUMMY

DICTIONARY

BANDAGES strips of cloth used to wrap up a body or a body part

CURSE a kind of magic spell that does something bad to a person

PRESERVED specially treated so it will not decay, or rot

SPELL a special saying that makes magic happen

TOMBS small rooms or holes in the ground where dead people are buried

23

MUMMIES

READ MORE

Besel, Jennifer M. *Mummies*. Mankato, Minn.: Capstone, 2007.

Carney, Elizabeth. *Mummies*. Washington, D.C.: National Geographic, 2009.

Hamilton, S. L. *Mummies*. Edina, Minn.: Abdo, 2011.

WEB SITES

FUNSCHOOL: HALLOWEEN

http://funschool.kaboose.com/fun-blaster/halloween/

This site has a lot of spooky games and pictures for coloring.

NATIONAL GEOGRAPHIC KIDS: TOMB OF THE UNKNOWN MUMMY

http://kids.nationalgeographic.com/kids/games/
interactiveadventures/tomb-unknown-mummy/

Learn more about mummies by exploring tombs in this game.

INDEX